# Alchemy

Diana Pinckney

*Diana, March 2004*

*For Craig,
Who knows how much
it means to keep the pages
turning. Best, Diana*

MAIN STREET RAG PUBLISHING COMPANY
CHARLOTTE, NC

Cover art: "Litchfield Reflections," acrylic on paper, by Elizabeth Barnes Pinckney

Acknowledgments

My gratitude to the editors of the following journals in which some of these poems, or earlier versions of them, first appeared:

*Asheville Poetry Review:* "Myrtle Court" and "So Drawn to the End"
*Iodine*: "After Spring Rain" and "Because my Grandmother Loved a Poet"
*Main Street Rag*: "How To Be," "On the Dock at Pawley's Island" and "When It's Over"
*Nebo*: "Behind the Kitchen Door"
*Southern Poetry Review*: "August 1945" and "Tiger Woods at Sawgrass"
*The Devil's Millhopper*: "If the Hospital Calls" -- Honorable Mention in the Sand River Poetry Contest for poems in forms
*The Sow's Ear Poetry Review*: " Blue Heat"

I am in debt to the community of North Carolina poets and editors that have supported and encouraged me. I'm fortunate to live in the midst of so many fine, caring writers. And I don't forget Mary Wilmer whose warmth and words graced us all. Thank you, Becky, Betty, Cathy, Dannye, Eleanor, Irene, Jonathan, Julie, Keith, Ken, Lou, Louise, Lucinda, Mary C., Maureen, Terri, Tootsie, Barbara C. and Barbara P., Dede, Gail and of course, Scott.

ISBN 1-930907-41-9

Published by
Main Street Rag
4416 Shea Lane
Charlotte, NC 28227
www.Main StreetRag.com

# Contents

*for Francis,*
*who always knows where we are*

*Every day our name is changed,*
  *say stones colliding into waves.*
*Go read our names on the shore,*
  *say waves colliding into stones ...*

*Before you read the farthest wave,*
  *before our shadows disappear*
*in a starry blur, call out your name*
  *to say where we are.*

— Colette Inez, "Lake Song"

# SEA ISLAND, GEORGIA

Summer hangs helpless and pale
from this thick sky. One state away

wildfires inhale whole forests in a breath
and smoke blurs the beach

we walk, here to celebrate
a marriage, counting years with sand and salt.

From brown fields
to the tops of pines, long needles

sizzling like sparklers, wind burns
hot enough to spin featherless babies

from their nests.
The day we married, my ivory dress

was heavy with lace and sweat,
your Navy whites trembled

at the altar. Like flames
from the roots of sawgrass,

we have widened the path,
follow it even now. How reckless

to think we could've made
each other happy, much less be kind,

or that we could come this far
and not find fire.

## BLUE HEAT

Winter was not done with us
the year the furnace burned out.
My father shoveled and stoked,
hauled no telling how many lumps of coal
to the living room hearth, blue heat
circling us like a happy family.

When he said, *We can't afford
a new furnace*, my mother's glare singed
the air for days. Curled under blankets,
Grandmother's quilts, any wool thing,
we took comfort from the dark sun
of my father's voice as he read to us

by the fire and my mother's refusal to huddle
or bundle. The ashes grew, gray mounds
consuming the cinders of a long damp March,
Mother promising, *You'll be warmer tomorrow,*

as if she could dig spring from the earth
the way her hands had worked the soil
in late fall, planting white marble bulbs
soon to torch purple and yellow
on the table. Though nothing changed
the weather in that house.

# WHEN ONLY FANS STIRRED THE AIR

We give in, leave our beds at two a.m., hauling quilts
        to the back lawn, the whole family sprawling
                on wide-bladed Charleston grass that crackles

with June bugs, my mother lamenting
        lost constellations, all of us searching
                for stars that won't fall, leaving the sky

to a transient moon, the night to the floating ember
        of my father's Lucky Strike, breath rough
                in his chest, his ruined heart already drowning.

# A PORCH BY THE OCEAN, THE FIFTH OF JULY

The shrimp we peel are pink, limp
    heads scattered like string and beads
        across a table covered in newspapers:

photos of a robot on Mars, its gray and red vistas
    under bowls of butterbeans, crowder peas,
        headlines awash in shells.

Passing wine and bread, we squeeze lemons,
    tell too many jokes, three couples treading the space
        left by a brother and two sisters

taken by scavenger cells. The rover Sojourner
    collects dust from rock and rivers of gravel
        on the planet high above the surf pounding nearby.

At the round table, we bury Mars under corncobs,
    pull our chairs close, stay until night spins into day,
        an unquenchable sun consuming the sky.

# AUGUST 1945

The week Hiroshima and Nagasaki turned
to smoke and ashes, I learned to swim
in mountain water so cold
my legs shivered and jerked.
At the edge of the lake, a lifeguard
held my face, scissored my limbs
until she let go and the only thing between

me and the green gummy bottom
was my own body burning like a motor.
One afternoon as we sputtered and flailed,
bells began. Stepping from the water
we saw a silent tide of women, my mother
among them, moving down the mossy path
from the Inn to the pine chapel

where candles licked the windows.
Some carried small black prayer books,
a few covered their heads with scarves,
all the faces wet as mine.
On the trail a red sun lit the mica
in the rocks and flamed the lake
with a fire that rippled in every direction.

## SO DRAWN TO THE END,

doomsday cults gather in caves
waiting to welcome it
then find the appointed day closing
with only the usual losses.

What familiar music the piper plays,
the high, slicing scream
of a lifeguard's whistle as we crowd
around what drifts in the pool.

And my grandmother at ninety-four
leaving us ounce by ounce until she thins
into a reedy voice asking,
*When will I get to the end of my row?*

We've seen the way
hunters love the light
passing from the eyes of deer,
how when the woods darken

we come home
watching for the highway's
harvest, all those quiet shapes
along the side.

# THE HOUSE ON ENOREE AVENUE

Charleston grass fading and winter rye
flashing green shoots along the flagstone,
my father's brown Chevrolet angled
in the drive too early,
the stairwell, a funnel pulling me up
past Grandmother hurrying down
from a bed that heaves
with my father, his eyes
a slash of brown sinking to black —
*A weight's on my chest*, he whispers,
my mother leaning down, *Try to be still, please* —
only the skim of her breath between them
until she straightens and steps away,
the siren outside —
Grandmother calling, *They're here* —
backs of men bent over the bed,
sheets, stretcher, my father's white face,
the van, my parents
swallowed up in the back, a blur
as it shrieks away, leaving us
in the front yard,
my deaf grandmother and me
beside a red cedar that will not change
except to drop a few berries in fall.

# OCTOBER CHILD

My daughter is jumping,
slick with wet fall leaves
that thicken the yellow air,

lungs gummy in her chest,
sticky as wet leaves falling,
my daughter wheezing,

chest thick with gummed lungs.
She pants in piles of crimson, gold.
I hear the wheezing.

Lips ringed with blue
swirl in gold, crimson
and she is ashes falling down.

We drive through rings of blue
rain, newly barren trees in lines of gray,
her ashen face sliding down

the seat. Cars back up
in rain, barren gray lines.
At last the entrance, mask,

syringe, people backing up
to let us through. Gasping girl
at last wearing her mask

that bubbles the yellow air,
loosens the glue. Adrenaline girl.
My daughter is jumping.

# MYRTLE COURT

(for *a man married to the same woman
all of his life*)

Crape myrtles draped the sidewalks
down your childhood street, blossoms
in the fountain's three tiers.

We coppered the circle on the bottom
with pennies we threw, believing it made
a difference. What swam

in our heads with such trust? And what
has time bought – who saved who?
Remember the argument

one election eve that lasted until love
at dawn? Not even the day's fine gold
stopped us from canceling each other's vote.

Now a cul-de-sac, the court holds
young families adding decks
to tile and stucco houses,

driveways wide with vans and jeeps.
Magenta petals stain the stones
where we climbed wet steps,

peering through all that spilled
to see what settled.

# HOW MY BROTHER SPENDS HIS DAYS

Does he shamble on bad ankles,
      room to room following her
            faint scent to the closet, silk arms

of blouses stirring when he cracks
      the door, or does he stand at the sink
            washing his hands over and over

the tiles she chose, a seafoam color
      like the ocean outside the condo, the tide
            leaving shell after shell as he is left

with photos covering every table,
      five decades of the two of them,
            a frame for every dawn he'll dream

of the house in Michigan, those grand foolish years
      he insisted on planting a magnolia
            or camellia, the relentless autumn air

dropping faster than he could dig,
      faster than they could lower the root-ball
            into frozen ground, her face smooth, enchanted

under a sweep of crystal blue that splinters
      as he wakes into waves breaking,
            gulls claiming the sky, screeching the news.

# BIRDS

My friend who died the nineteenth of October
        heard the white-throated sparrow
                float its song through the pines.

She lay in bed holding her son's hand,
        whispering the bird's name.
                Her son, puzzled: *But he always comes back*

*on the twenty-first*, for he had learned birds
        from her. And before turning to the window,
                she answered, *He's early.*

Now, in a rusted gutter
        above a window next to my desk —
                scrabble, peck. Long pauses as I work

uneasy, wondering
        when they'll move on,
                will they be back.

# WHEN IT'S OVER

We move on, like the Senator
on the six o'clock news,
fielding questions about the son
he hasn't seen for years,
arrested for dealing drugs.
Words fall from his mouth
that have long waited to be said.

Love never finishes with us:
the aunt who grows deaf and difficult
to visit comes to me now
in a stranger's plump hands,
the marriage that continues
under cover of divorce

or the dog I gave away
to a friend in the country.
Afternoons, when the drive
blurs gray, I think I see
that sleek black body,
one foot raised, nose in the air
the way the heart tracks
whatever has been lost.

# NIGHTSPOTTING

Our bearded Australian host opens a sock
where a musky-rat-kangaroo sleeps.
Light trembles through the rainforest
as he talks of sanctuary, the rescue
of flightless birds.

> Across the sea, our son walks two dogs
> before work, a leash in each hand,
> ball cap shading his eyes,
> the rebuilt nose almost straight

while we dine on lamb, potatoes and wine,
breathing eucalyptus from the garden's edge.
The host's wife strokes the wing of a fox-faced bat
that clutches her blouse, another in an apron pocket,
saying, *These are our children.*

> Weeks ago emergency door lights flared,
> people lined the halls like mannequins.
> *What have they done to him? Brass knuckles,*
> the policeman said, *maybe a fist of quarters.*

Apple cores, mango rinds on the lawn
draw a cassowary on tall legs, three toes
deep in the grass. His metallic helmet pierces
the twilight. Following the bird, two month-old chicks,
big as hens, stab at peels.

My son held towels against his face,
socks sagging with blood.
Next to him, his girl quivered
like a hummingbird on a string.

*The female lays them and leaves,* the Australian says.
The cassowary turns, leads his brood, head lowered,
black plumage into wet black foliage.
*Not enough forest for each male's turf.*

They had gone for groceries,
a parking lot hissing footsteps
and ugly words. He stepped back
between the girl and three young men,
his face turned to what was coming.

Fan palms rustle. Among the hibiscus
wallabies scoop blossoms from the grass,
limp flowers in their paws.
Our hostess says, *They come at dusk.*
Caught in the beam of flashlights,
eyes stare back like fractured stars.

# MAGDALENE
*Museo del Duomo*


The eyes shock me back to my mother
the night after her

surgery. In the bed where
her leg had been, a hollow.

Now this statue, Magdalene out of the desert,
out of a poplar's gnarled stump.

In a gallery of marble men,
a woman created from wood,

matted hair a web of worms
preserved in polychrome,

Magdalene waits
alone among stone-eyed saints.

In an agony of age, Donatello carved
this old Mary far from the grace

of forgiveness, her body and face honed
to brown bones, eyes like my mother's, looking

to the wall behind us, as if watching
something coming.

# A PLACE OF SEPARATION

She flutters between curb and sidewalk,
says she's slightly dizzy
when I fold her gauzy arm in mine.
Does gravity lessen with age,
the body preparing to leave,
hesitating above ground,
bones light as silk,
the world now closer
as it loosens its hold,
our attention freed
to see the veins of a leaf,
a caterpillar's yellow stripe
down the rosy stem,
the chrysalis green as Eden,
one thing becoming another.

# ELIZABETH PLAYS ALICE

Crossing a park at age eight,
hair long and blonde, my mother
heard a voice, *You're Alice, my Alice.*

*I'm Elizabeth*, she told the man.
But he directed the town theatre
and she played in Wonderland.

When an actor forgot his cue, little Alice
boomed the last line, called them all
*a pack of cards,* brought down the house.

Her mother took in boarders
and Alice resented strange hats in the hall,
the changing cups and faces at the table.

With callers by the dozen, she chose
my father who gave her a garden with thorns.
Alice, the queen of hearts in a full house

where her mother stayed the longest
leaving finally at ninety-four.
Alone, unable to stop the darkness

from climbing the bad foot,
Alice said, *Of all those gone,
I miss Mama most.* At her bedside no words,

no magic could keep her from growing
smaller in that room where the light stayed on
all night and she was gone by morning.

# THE INLET

Holding hands, three girls cross
   the inlet, wading at low tide.
      Seven, eight, ten

years old, the girls are breaking the rule,
   enchanted by the inlet at low tide.
      Minnows circle the ankles

of the girls breaking the rule.
   They leave the mainland,
      circles of minnows at their ankles.

Mothers call, then search, not knowing
   the girls have left the mainland,
      think they're shelling along the shore.

Others join the search, knowing
   sands shift and tides change
      covering shells and dunes along the shore.

Two girls dig on the island bank, one swims
   as the sea shifts, the tide changes,
      swelling the channel. A rosy sun dims behind

the girls on the island. Only one can swim.
   They rise, turn to go, leaving
      the channel island, its rosy sand behind.

The water churns, seven, eight, ten
   inches higher, turning, rising as they leave.
      The girls begin to cross, holding hands.

## AT THE BEACH, MY QUIET BROTHER,

who has loved the ocean all his life, tells me
he wants mountains. His wife died so suddenly,
only unknown hills move him. He will leave
the white sand, the waves tossing glints
of those quick small fish he's always tossing back
to a sea that gives up the moon at night.
Not speaking of her, never of two stillborn sons,
this childless man talks of woods and hollows,
thick with fog and loose black dirt,
rotting pine trails, mossy under sunlight
pale as mushrooms. And limestone,
cleft and chiseled, rising out of yesterday's shells.

## ALCHEMY

Don't tell the whole story
of the Captain's farewell dinner, eight strangers
at a round table, the wine steward's
black lipstick, how the food turned on me after

our words did, the next morning's silence
until a woman on the balcony beside ours
yelled, *Where is it written we have to be first
in line, front row on every tour?* and his answer

a slammed door.  We had no choice
but to laugh.  The Baltic
plucked at the stern,
its brown waters rendering amber
under the sun. And on the rail, your arm
caught in copper light.

# TIGER WOODS AT SAWGRASS

In nests round as washtubs, Great Blue herons
rock loblolly pines. A rookery over hole seven,

higher than the white balls
driven across lagoons and long greens.

Falling soundlessly, a ball rolls,
stops just short of the rippling flag. *Ohs*

and *Ahs* from the crowd while young herons
whir stumps of wings, small motors

on sticks, their cottony necks
looping overhead. To see them, we crane our necks

the way they throw back yellow beaks
and open for fish twice consumed, passed to these birds

from the parents who coast in, dinner
filling their crooked throats, starting an uproar

of clacking in the trees. Clubs crack like lightning.
The favorite, surrounded by bodyguards, leads

all of us to the next hole. The father,
who had dangled a golf iron before

his boy in a high chair, silent on the side. Above,
the fledglings clamor for more.

# AFTER SPRING RAIN

A tumor bubbles in a friend's brain —
this man whose mind twists
and turns the way a river
searches for its source.

As Mayor, he once replied to the lady
in the hat who asked
his position on massage parlors,
*Madame, I stand erect.*

*Afternoon ablutions,* he says now
when orderlies appear
to take him for his shower
of radium, daily burning of good and bad.

Flash of a cardinal's wing —
swooping my cat
who switches her tail, dreaming
a red fledgling from its nest.
Some find their way
through the dogwood's green.

# X RAY

*so called in 1895 because the discoverer
was uncertain of its nature*

Driving for treatments, she pictures
the flesh they cut from her breast,
pressed between glass like a botanical,
soft tissue that concealed the pebble
he discovered one dawn,
sun warming the sky,
the two of them chilled, leaving bed
and the outlines of bodies.

        Now with back and chest X'd
in bluish-red, divided into grids
the way a butcher separates a cow
then wraps the sections, she undresses
each morning, steps up to a steel table
where white heat beams above, the blowtorch
that will light her up inside.

        She remembers how as a girl
she slid both feet into the shoe machine,
the skeleton of toes glowed
vaporous below her
as if they belonged to another,
bones of ivory bamboo
planted in someone else's country.

## IF THE HOSPITAL CALLS

I plan to wear the tan skirt,
slip on sandals, the teal blouse.
Three times before, other nights,

I have left this house,
shot like a stone from a sling
into hot air under the slash

of moon, to the car, hood silvery
with dew, streets pale, quiet.
Now the clock that's in no hurry

flashes 3:06. Our bedroom fan cuts
minutes into hours, winding me
into your fluorescent nights, days on charts

that move in lines of red and green,
time a horizontal white that doesn't change.
People blur over your bed until it must seem

voices, faces are the same.
When the phone rings, I'll have planned it all --
reaching for glasses, keys and sweater because

sterile air is cold inside those walls.
If I lie still, they may not call.

# INVIITATION IN APRIL

Just the right tone, the voice
asking me to come in for a sonogram
of my left breast. Sonogram,

a small bomb in my ear.
How easy she makes it sound
and *easy* is what I tell myself, *easy,*

as I stare through a window
at white azaleas heavy with bumblebees.
*Are you writing this down?*

Well of course I'm writing it down,
questions humming a black buzz
in my head. *Isn't this a different place*

*from where I had the mammogram?*
*Yes, this is where the doctor will talk to you.*
I see someone in green, in glasses,

walking into a cool blue room where I'll sit, waiting.
I put down the phone, my desk
a swarm of meaningless clutter,

my body a stranger, dark and busy.

# BEHIND THE KITCHEN DOOR

is where the devil beats his wife
when sunshine strikes through rain.
Rosa said so. I sat twisting
pigtails she'd plaited, listening

to stories of a daughter my age.
She called her my twin
while I doodled with grits she served
from the black stove. Anytime

a beam flashed on wet windowpanes,
I hopped from stool to kitchen door
to catch Satan in mid-blow
sure that Rosa would protect me.

Six States and years away
I held my own baby girl
and listened to my mother keen
across the miles. Rosa's girl,

she said, dead. My darker sister
shot in Rosa's yard,
flung like a doll on the front stoop,
Rosa rushing out,

the young man yelling, *See what I done
to your baby*? In court,
when sentenced, he turned, swore
to come back and do the same

to Rosa. To Rosa, Rosa
who knew what waits
behind a door, knew what falls
is not always rain.

# TENNESSEE

*How do you know his women so well?*
my freshman English professor asked,
skeptical of my paper about the faded
beauties who languished then blazed

on Thomas Lanier Williams' stage,
the Amandas and Blanches —
that familiar parade -- my mother
descending the stairs in tears over my brother,

*gone, gone forever*. Forever
until his return from four years
in a peacetime Air Force. Mother burning
down the phone lines when an ex-boyfriend

dared to call the summer
he broke my heart. Mother
with the untamed cat that lived
on the mantelpiece, a dog that chewed

Persian rugs and pennies, the menagerie
of tipsy friends who presented avocados
at seven a.m., grapefruit at sundown
with their bruises and soft spots.

Mother wobbling on crippled legs
to show an intruder out, a man who came in
through her bathroom window. He left
by the back door he told her to be sure to lock.

After she dies, I find a snapshot
in her bedside drawer. A World War I pilot,
a dim, angular stranger,
not nearly so handsome as my dark-haired father.

# BECAUSE MY GRANDMOTHER LOVED A POET

I've found a book of Sir Walter Scott's
collected works, inscribed in brown ink
with the name, *Morgan Brown Thompson*,
and under that, *Lizzie Fearn Eldridge*, 1893.
And because he died of tuberculosis
the year they became engaged,
Morgan Brown Thompson was not my grandfather.
The family said my grandmother went to live
with his parents and wore black for a year.

I see her twist her long auburn hair and pin it
in the back before she rides her horse
so furiously through the Virginia countryside,
home by dawn to keep her own father's house,
until finally she marries a widower,
a scholar, they say. She referred to him
as Mr. Barnes. Did he call her Lizzie?
Recite Shakespeare's sonnets to her?

Years later my grandmother stepped
from a deaf world and crossed the hall
to help me dress for that lovely boy
waiting at the bottom of the stairs.
Where in these split covers and shoebox letters
I sort now, are those poems he wrote to me?
The musty dust of first love thickens the air
while my keep-stack grows,
pages peeling, spines exposed.

# ON THE DOCK AT PAWLEY'S ISLAND

Her brush pulls the sun
across canvas. She paints a creek shrinking

at low tide, wood bedded
in oyster shells. *Thirty years*, I say,

*since you've been here, since we crabbed.*
*Tying those smelly chicken necks to sticks.*

*And the bucket that turned over*
*on the porch?* We laugh, swirl

again into that rush, blue claws
scratching, aunts leaping onto chairs.

Earlier, I drove her past land sold
for steak houses and mini-golf.

Unforgiving of all that shifts
memory's landscape, we forget

what the sea remembers,
inching the coastline toward old ground,

returning the way our minds comb
the topography of the past —

looking for dunes high as houses,
sea oats bent with blackbirds,

ghost crabs slipping down their holes.

## HOW TO BE

In the ocean, our flowered suits billowing
around us, I ask my friend how to be
a grandmother. I, who have lived
on the curve of a question mark,
never certain what to do for my children
except tell them stories and wrap
blankets around their solitary bodies
pulled into tight balls, knees drawn up,
fists closed against whatever
cold is coming. So I ask,
confessing I am sure of one thing only —
I will read to the one now filling
my daughter-in-law's loose dresses,
but what else? *Go outside together,*
my friend tells me, *turn over a rock,*
*count the roly-polies.* Yes, of course,
and I lean back into salt-water swells.

# A WINTER MOON,

forked by an oak's branches,
pearls across my dresser,
skimming your pillow.

Where are the nightmares
we woke each other from,
the *noes* and *yeses* of this bed.

Tonight on television a former
activist, recalling the revolutions
of his life, said to the interviewer,

*Nothing makes me mad anymore.*
Chaplin-like, he sauntered away,
his back to lights, cameras,

questions, the world
grown too absurd to take
his breath or stop it.

Did he stroll out
into a moonless night,
has he forgotten that in summer

a ripe melon hangs over the ocean
spilling milk-white
across old cots on old porches

like the one we once lay on
mouthing every desire.